This Heart

*For Ari Aneurin and Leo Starling Cariad
and the poetry that brings you here*

This Heart

Poems from the universe inside

Martin Wroe

wild goose publications

www.ionabooks.com

Copyright © Martin Wroe 2025

First published 2025 by
Wild Goose Publications
Suite 9, Fairfield, 1048 Govan Road, Glasgow G51 4XS, Scotland
A division of Iona Community Trading CIC
Limited Company Reg. No. SC156678
www.ionabooks.com

ISBN 978-1-80432-382-3

Cover painting © Malcolm Doney. Cover design © Jeff Fisher.

All rights reserved. Apart from the circumstances described below relating to non-commercial use, no part of this publication may be reproduced in any form or by any means, including photocopying or any information storage or retrieval system, without written permission from the publisher via PLSclear.com.

Non-commercial use:
The material in this book may be used non-commercially for group work without written permission from the publisher. If photocopies of sections are made, please make full acknowledgement of the source, and report usage to CLA or other copyright organisation.

Martin Wroe has asserted his right in accordance with the Copyright, Designs and Patents Act, 1988, to be identified as the author of this work.

Overseas distribution
Australia: Willow Connection Pty Ltd, 1/13 Kell Mather Drive, Lennox Head NSW 2478
New Zealand: Pleroma, Higginson Street, Otane 4170, Central Hawkes Bay

Printed in the UK by Page Bros (Norwich) Ltd

	MIX
FSC www.fsc.org	Paper	Supporting responsible forestry FSC® C023114

This heart

This heart   10
This heart that holds a universe   11

This now

Terra Divina (William Blake remix)   14
Robin   15
Blackbird   15
Swallow   16
Parliament   16
And also with you   17
Nature poem   18
Iceberg   19
I never knew   20
Glorious weather   21
The end of myself   22
Surround sound   23
Tent   24

This here

It arrives   28
Noises off   29
Pane   30
Location   31
Now   32
'Vast new reserves discovered'   33
Grumbling   35
Here's the thing   36
Everyday election   37
No charge   38

6　This heart

Rhythm with blues　39
Detectorist　40
Each day　41
You are being held in a queue　42

This love
Everyone a candle　46
First person (Poem on Mother's Day)　47
Old friends　48
Call the midwife　50
My third marriage　51
If you liked this …　53
Being there　54
Who's Elvis?　55
Legacy　56
Assemble　57
I would love to live　58

This way
Prayer heard outside court at the immigration hearing　62
The repair shop　63
On guard　64
Out in the back　65
The squeeze　66
Bubble　67
Product recall　68
Thoughts and prayers　69
Sink　70
Poem started on a birthday　71
Taking my prayers for a walk　72

This story

Tradition   74
Fear not   75
The book   76
Gazing at a star (Christmas poem)   77
Ring out the old   78
Spiritual not religious   79
Epiphany   80
How to become an insider   81
Forty (Poem in Lent)   83
easter revolution   84
Church noticeboards   86
Priest   87
Retreat   89
The day the weeks meet   90
More   92

This end

A quiet word   94
Elastic snap   96
Spring   97
Taking mum to the doctor   97
Hazardous   98
One in the morning   99
Home from home   100
My back has gone   102
Affronted   103
What are we going to do?   104
Unlock   105
Lowering   106
Same seat as you   107

Seven blessings when you lose someone you love
(A funeral poem)   108
Alive   110
Scattering   111
The light we shared (A parting poem)   112
Fall   113
Gone   113
Sign of the peace   114

This home
Life writing   116
Catch   116
Why the rule?   117
Stand   118
Candle   119
Warmth   120
The fix   120
Guidance   121
This is a poem about death   122
Almost nothing   123
Life; a customer satisfaction survey   124
Call it   126
Psalm 23 (remix)   127
(Psalm for a) home   128
Listen now!   129
Thankful   130

This life (Some afterwords)   131

Sources and acknowledgements   137

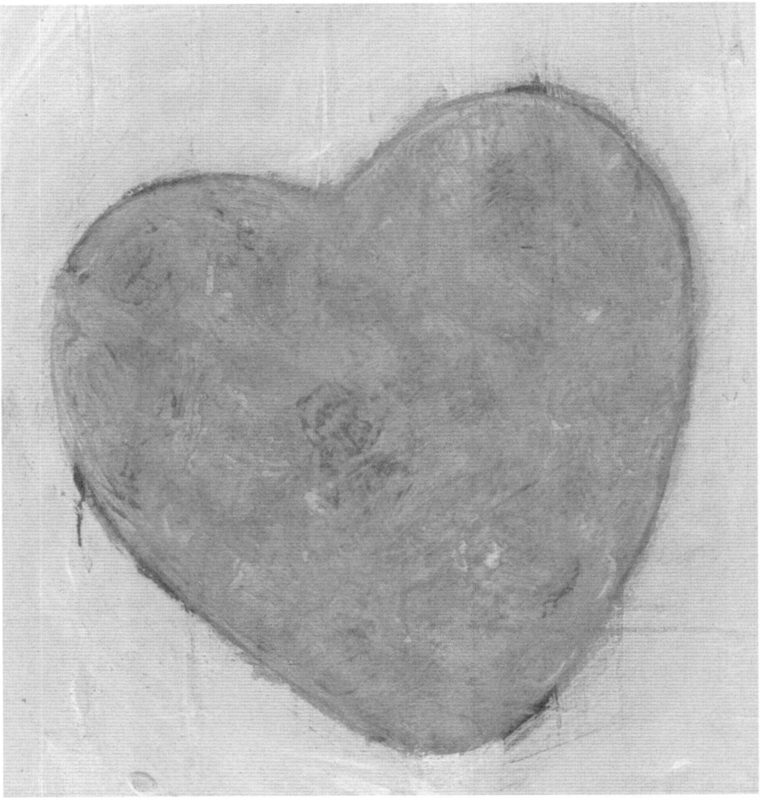

This heart

This heart is portable
I take it wherever I go
This heart cannot move
It is anchored to you

This heart is on my sleeve
And more than it appears
This heart is all unseen
And all you see of me

This heart is at capacity
Standing room only
This heart is wall to wall
With room for one more

This heart does not exist
This heart is a metaphor
This heart is a poem
The truest thing of all

This heart that holds a universe

Poetry is the language that many of us don't know we speak. The rhyme and rhythm of a familiar story that we've never heard before.

Writing, reading or listening to poetry introduces the universe inside us to the universe outside and helps them get to know each other. The poems in this book arrived when something inside me started knocking on the door of something outside and found that the door was already open.

The trees in the breeze bowing to each other. That song about you on the radio. The cyclist pedalling through the air. A robin looking up at you as if you'd asked a question.

Most of these poems found themselves early in the day in my quiet time at a local coffee shop, the moment when I try to slow life down to find my place in it. The naive attempt to snap a photo of time as it passes, not dissimilar to the act of reflection sometimes called prayer. Most days I find these two, poetry and prayer, falling into each other's arms.

Poem, prayer, psalm, song, all the same exercise in getting silence to cough up its truth. To persuade meaning to compromise a little, to give an inch. To stop being so mysterious.

Perhaps the poem already exists and even now is winking at you, waiting to explain your life. Or maybe it's bluffing. Perhaps it was buried a million years ago and has been waiting for someone to dig it up, now that it's out of copyright.

The ancient traditions in the poetry of faith can feel less resonant in offering shape to a life but the everyday baffle in the soul that gives rise to those practices has not gone anywhere. The loose shape of this volume – from noticing we are here to accepting we have to leave – responds to the same bafflement.

Poems are practical, a language to explain ourselves to each other, a lens through which to see a day differently.

Poems are not monuments to visit on a poetry trip but the robin looking at you from the garden, ready to answer your question.

'This heart is a poem
The truest thing of all'

THIS NOW

Terra Divina (William Blake remix)

Lectio

Several hundred billion years
In this crumbling fistful of sand
Slipping through fingers, back to earth
Infinity in the palm of my hand

Meditatio

Rocks and pebbles, shells and sand
Hold eternity in an hour
Inhaling space, swallowing time
Slo-mo miracle, superpower

Oratio

Thank you, grass, thank you, earth
In the future we'll get together
The world in a grain of sand we'll find
And how now is also for ever

Contemplatio

One day in the distance, weathered and worn
Someone will hold us in their hand
An extremely old version of you and me
Now inhabiting that grain of sand

Robin

Just me, my pen, this coffee
Waiting on the mystery
A robin descends from a tree
Perches here, looking at me
Then rises, into the breeze
Says, I'll be your poetry

Blackbird

Deep-buried thought, shy of the light
Blackbird drops by, out of the sky
Buttercup beak, yellow-ringed eye
Studying me, as if I know why
We consider the light
In each other's eyes

Swallow

Sitting, distracted, blank page, no lines
A blur in the air, orange and blue design
Visitor arrives, after 8000 miles
Supersonic flight to this nest in the heights
Leaps off this page, says
Come and ride these skies

Parliament

In the Parliament of Rooks
They were debating
The Murder of Crows
With all the Mischief of Magpies
When a Band of Jays struck up
And the entire motion was
Up in the air again

And also with you

If I had not made time
Earlier today, to pause
In the breeze, to be still
Among that small company of trees
I would not have noticed
How they were all bowing,
Shyly, to each other
I would not have heard
One of them whispering
Through the leaves,
'Let us share a sign of the peace'
(I'm sure that's what I heard)
And then the chorused refrain
'Peace be with you.'

'And also with you,'
I replied
To all of them, and also
And also, and also
With you

Nature poem

Late in the summer a river of people is rolling out of the stadium
I am carried in the flow
The morning after and along the pavement a couple approach
Talking,
I am silent as their voices rise
She is listening quietly as he says that this thing
Could be something that could be cancer
I am more silent still
Now that they have passed
I think how soon autumn arrives, then winter

Sitting outside Bluebell, a coffee shop on Holloway Road
The clouds hang briefly in the cold morning
As another is exhaled from the table next to me
Hanging there existentially
Before rising and disappearing
Without answering the question it was raising

A crocodile of Year 4 children in blue and yellow shirts
Slalom by, a spaniel in a pink raincoat
Looks with longing towards a woman
Who believes she owns him
She passes him some of her toast
and draws deeply on her cigarette, phone shouldered
To ear, hands dropped
To her side, where they trail
More clouds of glory

Here on the water's edge I see everyone
Entangled deep in the soil of for ever
Branches reaching up into deep space
None of us aware of the invisible root system
Through which we all sustain each other

Francis, who I have only ever met once,
Tells me in the flow people were hugging him,
People he had never met
I said they were hugging me too
I picture him, carried like me, in the river

Iceberg

When there is no longer a
Tip of the iceberg
We will know there is no iceberg
And that this is no longer just
The tip of the iceberg

I never knew

I never knew the trees were
Speaking to each other out of sight

Or how Hildegard could know
They make energy from light

Or that the green earth is conscious
Is breathing, is alive

That there are ecosystems of hope
Inside this wild entangled life

I never knew we were relatives
The sun, the moon, the sea, the sky

I never knew we were stardust
You and me, blown into time

Until I learned to speak
In the language of leaves

The one they sing together
As a breeze blows in the trees

Glorious weather

Can you believe this glorious weather?
Is it still summer if it goes on for ever?

The garden's green grass is already brown
Horse chestnut leaves all coming down

Under the lid the compost bin's on fire,
Concealing the flames of our own funeral pyre

Headlines predict we're in for a scorcher
Can't sit outside, the temperature's torture

Strip off, come on in, the water's lovely
Temperatures risen by two degrees C

Another nice day, you wince at the phrase
Elsewhere in the world, the end of days

What is the word, the Germans must have it
That feeling of joy which gives way to calamity

There goes your car sailing down the street
Where's Noah and his Ark in the Anthropocene

Fossil fuels flow, hose pipes are banned
No cause for alarm, you've got a nice tan

Seasonal breakdown, nature in therapy
Habitat destruction, climate catastrophe

Lock up the heretics for a very long time
They've lost all perspective, they're out of their minds

The sixth great extinction, frogs in the pot
Which explains why this poem's a little agitprop

The end of myself

The print on the end of this finger
Does not mark the end of me

The epidermis is only a beginning
It does not contain you

We are beyond ourselves
As well as inside ourselves

We are an out-of-body experience
So that this thought,
Somewhere in my time and space,
Is greeting your thought
Somewhere in yours
Even though I'm not with you,
Whoever you are,
But also I am

When I reach the end of myself I find you

Surround sound

The maritime pines look down from on high
Silent surround sound, silhouetting the sky

Over the hill yawns the wind from the sea
The maritime pines are shooting the breeze

Standing beside us, taking the pressure
The maritime signs are reading the weather

Drawing on hidden depth, reaching for light
Companions beside us, by day and by night

Steady and calm, anchored in earth
You turn, they're present, always just here

Faith, hope and love surround every day
Circle of protection, ancient embrace

Tent

We lie on the floor
And feel the bend of the earth
In the crook of our back
This canvas womb is warm in parts
But also moist
And there is a persistent draught

The music calls us and, as it's two a.m.,
Perhaps it could stop
We are nature, lying in nature
When nature calls
A field of wheezing *zzzzzs*
And squealing *zzzzzs*,
The zip on the tent next door

We lie in the dark
On this great hidden plain of dreaming
Dawn breaks, the cattle are lowing,
A baby awakes (crying she makes)
In pyjamas we queue for a shower
Or hang a head under a tap of cold water
Quietly asking ourselves
If we are still doing this

We are nomads camped on a long journey
This stop is familiar
As if we have been here before
As if we are travelling in circles

But we are not lost
Except to the people we once were
And every time we pitch up on this ground
Bend again to this good earth
We find a little more of ourselves
And become a little more less lost

THIS HERE

It arrives

It arrives with an annoying email you wish you hadn't read
It arrives with the thought that you do not have to let
   annoying emails annoy you
It arrives with a reminder of that sadness
It arrives with light pouring in through the window
   as you pull back the curtain
It arrives with the thought of that call you don't want to make
It arrives with the memory that you bottled out of it yesterday
It arrives as you replay that goal
It arrives with a small bird landing on the TV aerial of the house
   over the street
It arrives as the sky looks back at you, asking you
   what your problem is
It arrives as a shower wakes up your head
It arrives as you put away the dishes and wait for the kettle
   to boil
It arrives as you stand there noticing your own breath
It arrives in one still moment
It arrives with gratitude
It arrives
It arrives
It arrives

Noises off

Kettle boils, off it clicks
Sparrows garden gossip
Fridge whirrs, growls, hums
Woodpecker on the drums
Floorboard somewhere creaking
Distant siren screaming
Stream of thought that's bubbling
The hopeful and the troubling
This breath that calls to stillness
This heart that holds a universe
This fleeting understanding
That both are still expanding

Pane

First thing, at my desk, sitting down
I look towards two panes of glass
Two windows into new worlds
Each crossed and lined with greeting
Openings in light

Through one I see a tree,
Waving, maybe at me
Grey rooftops darkened by rain
Blue skies disguised in grey
Feels like we're meant to speak
But none has a word for me

After this moment of
Missing each other
(I am usually hurrying on to a receding future)
I turn from that pane
To this one
From where I make these crosses and lines
And speak to you now

Location

As each new trip begins
And I'm asked if it's OK
To use my location
Just now
Or always
To place me on the map
In all of this, in all the days

I want to recall
That earlier this morning
Briefly, I was still
And this still stilled everything
I want to say yes
This is my location
The place I come from today

Now

Next time is next time
Now is now
Stop what you're doing
We're all here ... somehow

Feel it, receive it
Look up, look down
Take it all in
Look all around

Receive this present
No need to ask how
Next time is next time
Now is now

'Vast new reserves discovered'*

Vast new reserves have been discovered
which could transform the way we live.
These untapped deposits
created by mysterious seismic movements,
deep below the surface,
are thought to have lain hidden since before
recorded time began.
Scientists believe that unusual stress near fault lines
forces them within human access and,
with a minimal refining process,
they may provide an unprecedented source of fuel for life.

The discovery was made in the course of research
into previously observed reserves of a substance called patience.
These deposits now turn out to be richer, deeper and more
pure than previously anticipated.
Alongside them, vast reserves of other energy sources have also
been located.
Gentleness, compassion, self-control and humility are thought
to be those with the greatest potential.

Experts speculate that while such substances
have been known to be present within certain individuals
throughout history,
it now appears they exist deep within everyone.
While the burning of traditional fuel sources like envy, greed
and vanity
provide excellent short-term results
in the form of an instantaneous rush of energy with an
immediate and satisfying hit,

34   This heart

a growing body of evidence now confirms unanticipated
side effects.
In fact, as more of us get hot under the collar, the entire globe
appears to be warming up, posing the possibility that the world
will become uninhabitable.

By contrast analysis of these new reserves suggests that
while they take longer to fire up
they do not burn themselves out
and are a sustainable, perhaps even endless,
source of power
which could supply humanity with essential resources
for generations.

But while these new reserves could transform
the human economy,
the process of extraction is not simple
and generally requires a period of training
which may take as long as a life.

Newspaper headline

Grumbling

Bone-weary and weather-worn
At the end of the island pilgrimage
Twenty of us, slumped, eyes closed
In the overgrown hillside ruins
Of the Hermit's Cell when, carried
On the breeze, from a hundred yards
And a thousand years away, a voice,
In the wilderness, grumbling,
'Every bloody week it's the same.
Will you please go away?
I didn't come here for company.'

Here's the thing

Here's the thing
There's never just the thing
Also, it turns out
No-one knows
How it turns out
And, by the way
No-one knows
What's round the corner
You go round it
There's another corner

Everyday election

The ballot box of being alive
The polling station of life
The vote of thanks for freedom
The mark we make on time

The dreams of those unlistened to
The worlds that we don't know
Those we choose to stand with
Each unpublished manifesto

Communities we invest in
Corporations we pass on by
The decision to be difficult
The brand we choose not to buy

The joy that won't be quantified
The dappled light in a tree
The stock exchange of kindness
Every hidden economy

How we travel these days on earth
Our compass and direction
The unseen world we look for
In the everyday election

No charge

The coins jangle in purse or pocket
The notes turn up in old books
You pass them to someone to pay a charge
They never need charging up

They will not notify you with a ping
If you're heading into the red
You cannot use them to send a text
But nor will they wake you in bed

The tap is not tactile, has no feeling
Contactless, no human touch
This genius, weightless trick of the light
'Sorry, mate, I've got no cash.'

Rhythm with blues

Woke up this morning
It was three a.m.
Lay there wide awake
Like the middle of the day

Slept through breakfast
Woke in a state
Left my body
In some other place

Day thinks it's night
Night thinks it's day
Three coffees later
Dropping off again

Biological clock
All tick, no tock
Mind won't stop
All wound up

Do I give up?
Do I push through?
These is my circadian
Rhythm and blues

Detectorist

Setting out once more
I move impatiently
Over this weathered terrain
Then remind myself

To slow
And now, to stop,
At this faint signal
This buried sound

Trowelling the dusty surface
I carry my doubt
That anything might be concealed
That hasn't been found
A hundred times before

Still, kneeling, I must believe
And dig up this shape,
Reach for its curve
And heft, weigh it up
Blow off the dust
It hasn't been moved
In a long time, it is worn
Beyond understanding

I lay it down, rise,
Move on
I believe there is a poem
Buried in this field
That when I slow down
I will find it

Each day

Each day is a quandary
A decision waiting for you
Each day unfinished story
That thing you don't want to do

Each day brings a message
You wish you hadn't read
Each day asks for courage
To face your feelings of dread

Each day is a puzzle
A problem that won't be solved
Each day there's that person
Asking to be loved

Each day a shock to the system
Insult or slap in the face
Each day some small wisdom
A smile, a warm embrace

Each day is inestimable
Stranger than we can predict
Each day someone, somewhere
Is also going through this

Each day is a stranger
Waiting to be introduced
Each day is a prayer
The one that cannot be said

You are being held in a queue

Will ticket number 37 please go to room number 11?
Please choose from the following four options.
Your call is important to us.
Please use contactless or insert your card.
Currently all of our agents are occupied.
Please follow the instructions on the card reader.
Our current wait time is forty-five minutes.
Will ticket number 114 please go to room number 18?
We wish you a safe and pleasant onward journey.
You are being held in a queue and will be answered shortly.
Please wait, an assistant is coming.
Please choose from the following twelve options.
Will ticket number 278 please go to room number 97?
Please wait for an assistant to confirm your age.
Thank you for shopping at Lidl.
Please be aware, calls may be recorded for training and
  quality purposes.
You are currently number 75 in the queue.
Please ensure you are travelling in the correct part of the train.
Unattended luggage may be removed or destroyed by the
  security services.
Stand well back from the platform edge.
The driver has been told to wait here to even out the service.
Thank you for shopping at Waitrose.
You are currently number 236 in the queue.
Your call is important to us.

Please choose from the following eight hundred options.
Please mind the gap between the train and the platform edge.
Ticket hall level. Please have your tickets ready.
We wish you a safe and pleasant onward journey.
Our current wait time is two days, six hours and
    forty-five minutes.
Please hold, we will be with you shortly.
We are experiencing a high volume of calls today.
You are number 9,337 in the queue.
Please choose from the following two thousand five hundred
    options.
Thank you for your call.
You are being held in a queue.
Please wait.
Please wait.

THIS LOVE

Everyone a candle

Everyone a candle
Blinking in the dark
All of us a torch
Light along the path

Everyone a cathedral
Listening for a song
All of us a prayer
Reverie and icon

Each encounter sacred
In person or on text
All this life a pilgrimage
To find everyone else

First person (Poem on Mother's Day)

The first person I ever found myself in
Before I knew
How to be found in someone

The first arms I was ever held in
Before I knew
What to be held was

The first face I ever saw
Before I knew
The face of love

Old friends

'Ah! Matisse. Oh! Cezanne'
We turn the corner, another room
Seeing a painting – '*The Umbrellas* – Renoir!' –
Or greeting a painter – 'Modigliani – aha!' –
Is running into old friends.
Ones the painter has been talking with
For most of her life

'Hello, Paul Klee, how are you?'
'And, Monet, of course, how could I forget?
I know you from London, Waterloo Bridge'
Van Gogh and Gauguin are speaking
With each other across the room
As we walk in, this painter joins in,
Across the centuries
It was only I had not realised
Her friendship with them
Began before we arrived

Sometimes a pause, a turn to me
'Do you know Georgia O'Keefe?'
Another friend, to stop and greet
'And have you met Seurat?'
Adding, under her breath
(Double-checking perhaps that he won't overhear)
'Pointillism does not mean he was neurodiverse.'

This foreign place where I don't speak the language
The shapes, movement, colour of this pilgrimage
Eavesdropping conversations which escape every frame
Bypassing words in this other domain
They're all lost to each other, in a way I can't read
Witness my question, as we prepare to leave
'I'm not sure,' she replies, 'if there is any more …'
No, actually, I'd asked, 'Is that a Henry Moore?'

Call the midwife

In the National Gallery in the City of Edinburgh
A saint goes first class from Iona to Bethlehem
A mediaeval journey, you can see the old Abbey,
Carried on angel wings en route to the Nativity

The cattle are lowing, even the donkey's in despair
Mary puts her mind deep inside a prayer
She calls the midwife, from somewhere else in history
No one keeps a record of maternal immortality

The flight takes off long after she has died
What's a few hundred years when you're Bridget of the Isles
Touchdown comes long before she is born
Normal rules don't apply when you're welcoming God's own

Way down below sounds a ringing of bells
As brush, paint and palette become the Book of Kells
Illuminated painting, the one we're all in
Even Mary can't tell what a prayer will begin

They break into stories that they were never in
And when winter's over they may announce spring
Brushing off laws of space and time
Next stop may be your place, next stop may be mine

Friends who are gone now, into the night
All the holy darkness that obscures our sight
Still they may carry us on impossible flights
Another kind of history, another kind of light

My third marriage

You said I do, I said I will
We meant it then, we mean it still
We didn't know what age would change
We are not who we were that day

I look at you, you look at me
Am I still who I used to be?
You know my best, you know my worst
When I'm blessed and when I'm cursed

We saw each other through the kids
If you do that, then I'll do this
The hours of a day insufficient
The altar's gaze intermittent

We lost each other more than once
It wasn't weeks, it wasn't months
Was it over, done and dusted
The altar's gaze interrupted

I tend to get moody, even dark
My light goes out, barely a spark
Eventually I will come back
You wait for me, this is our pact

I found a call and you found yours
Became ourselves, became some more
I'm not quite who I was that day
Perhaps we need to get married again

This heart

We're on our third marriage, maybe fourth
Up to now without a divorce
One day catastrophe, another epiphany
The altar's gaze is no guarantee

I look at you, you look at me
Can you still see who I used to be?
These faces written with joy and pain
We'll never meet first time again

For better, for worse, sickness and health
The light and dark arrive by stealth
We slowly come to work out how
Love and forgiveness our only vow

If you liked this ...

When I need to decide
What to watch next, or read
Or where to go
I have an algorithm I turn to
Which knows me well by now
Which understands my life stage and even
Seems to read my mood
My algorithm has seen everything
And tells me, sharing its excitement about a band or play
(Even pausing to reset, remembering
I can't do horror before bed)
The algorithm reels off a film scene, or recounts a line
   in a poem,
Then stares into the middle distance
At some remembered happiness
Now the algorithm's crying
I think you'd love this, she sobs
Still lost in her own world
Forgetting I'm here, then, maybe, a little insecure
I'm not sure if this is you, but I loved it
I sometimes wish my algorithm
Could be more efficient or less opinionated
And I must admit she's sometimes quite wrong
But then, I only built her by accident
I had no idea what I was doing
With all the rules I gave her, the programming
Over the kitchen table, in the pub

But as I followed her good taste, and took her advice
She solved so many problems
That I forgave her when she got it wrong
In the end
To be honest
My algorithm was just a good friend.

Being there

We may not need a plan
Or words to fit the moment
We may not need to have advice
Or even break the silence
We may need to do nothing
Except to see and hear
But being there
For someone else
We may find we are there
For ourselves

Who's Elvis?

The one the eyes are drawn to
Whose people made the list
Wrote our names down
In the centre of the crowd
That everyone gathers around

Who's Elvis in the room
That shrinks
When Elvis is gone?

The one you never see
Or look away from
Serving you your drink
Or on the edge of it all

Or doesn't look the part
Their invite, human error
Giving you a hard time
Doesn't seem to mind

Who's Elvis when Elvis
Has left the building?

Who's God
When
God is in the house?

Legacy

Some of us are on send
And never on receive
And fail to tune in
To you or me

They tell you it all
We're meant to be pleased
Doing this, doing that
Don't interrupt, you can't compete

The work and home, the great ideas
Amazing kids, what a family
No pause for breath, no thought of you
Let's call it nerves, or anxiety

It's all of us
On different days
Beaming out signals
Lost in space

Saying we're here
Proving we exist
Scratching our legacy
On the cave wall of eternity

Assemble

To assemble ourselves, from the flat pack of life
Respect, equality, kindness, insight
To design a politics of love not hate
To read freedom and dignity in every face

To hold complexity in the palm of your hand
Some injustice, conundrum, community plan
To open your mind as it's described to you
To speak from the heart, from your point of view

From no trust in power to the power of trust
The power in asking, who hasn't spoken yet?
A space designed to hear everyone else
Where a mind, even mine, might change itself

Truth does not fall in tablets from on high
It arrives on the quiet as we organise
As we enter the story of each other's lives
And slowly the revolution is decentralised

I would love to live

For Jean Willson

'I would love to live
As a river flows
Carried by the surprise
Of its own unfolding.'
(From 'Fluent', by John O'Donohue)

I would love to live
Like the day's first coffee
Rewiring this brain
With unknown possibility

I would love to live
Like a child new to cycling
Already forgotten that balance
Was once so frightening

I would love to live
With the gardeners' trust in the buried seed
Certain we will grow
Into all the light we need

I would love to live
As if every face mirrored dignity
Kindness, solidarity, joy
Reflecting it back to me

I would love to live
Like the potter at the wheel
Feeling for the shape
That one day I will see

I would love to live
As if nothing was impossible
Each new hostility or prejudice
Just one more obstacle

I would love to live
Like a big night out on the town
Then rest, rest, rest in peace
Tired, happy and home

I would love to live
As if the tears of those we leave
Are an ocean of love and friendship
Some clue to life's mystery

THIS WAY

Prayer heard outside court at the immigration hearing

'Oh Jesus Christ,
Does that mean
We've got to come back
Here again?'

The repair shop

Look at us all, malfunctioning, remaindered
Casualties of our history
Embarrassed to find ourselves
On display like this

You, defeated, blood on your forehead,
Spreading like a map across your blouse

You, wired, running at three times normal speed
Jumping up and down from your seat, needing to be
   dialled down

You, looking for the paperwork. (Are the instructions in
   your handbag?)
You always knew how it worked. (They're here somewhere.)

And you, leg elevated on the next seat, looking at me,
   in this wheelchair
We who were recently both so effortlessly mobile.

Look at us.
Caught out by time (at least four hours when I last asked)
Pushed too hard, until the pressure broke us
Neglected, until no-one could remember how we had
   once worked

Every body broken.
Doubting we could ever be good as new.

On guard

We are all of us soft
You do know that, don't you?
Under this armour we put on –
eyes that scan, balled
fists to repel each other,
defence mechanisms we manufactured early –
underneath this is the scar
tissue, the hidden tender.

Listen closely, how that unwavering
Voice trembles with some
Gentler word
Often unheard
Usually scared
I'm tired of being on guard
This is what it says
Can I put these weapons down?

Out in the back

I put it down, out in the back
There is a corner, out of sight
A storage space, a little stack
I'll return when the time is right

The casualties in this new war
Children who shiver in boats
The rising tides and forest fires
The death of someone I loved

Some days a kind of closing down
A new visitation of dread
The thought that shakes the very ground
Pick it up, put it by the rest

Some nights they're out, make their escape
In the morning they hunt me down
A haunting of this world we've made
These thoughts that go round and round

I'll go today, I won't forget
Maybe you could be at my side
I'll shine a light, I'll talk with them
In the corner at the back of my mind

The squeeze

You tighten your grip, it loosens again
Then tight as the judge names the crime
Knuckles bending, fingers outstretched
The stress ball, like justice, is blind

Your expanding universe of fear and dread
Disappears, deep into your palm
All that keeps you awake at night
Compressed in this ball of calm

The panic recedes, a quiet arrives
Squeezed out of this tiny sphere
Haunted by days in all the wrong places
Scenes you can never unsee

Fraudster or thief, innocent or guilty
Who else squeezed this world in their hand?
Who else, their days held in the balance,
Found some way to breathe on the stand?

No one but you knows the journey you've taken
All those who abandoned your ship
Hold on in the storm, even in this dock
Another universe firm in your grip

Bubble

My prayers were once all speech bubble
Texting information to a place where
No one needs informing
Because everything is known
Now, more often, they are the bubbles
Before the speech
The bubbles with the dots which say
This prayer is being formed
Before the dots stop and the bubble is gone

Product recall

I would like to recall my previous self
I would like to remove that version of me from the market
Significant consumer responses indicate a series of faults
I was not ready for public adoption
I was not able to perform as promised
On some occasions, I confess, I may have become a risk
   to public safety
I would like to recall my previous self

In a competitive environment I came to market too soon
I was not ready for public testing
I will address audience feedback in installing upgrades
I appreciate the reputational risk and loss of market share but
with modifications I will turn this around

If you have already invested in this earlier version of me
you will be eligible for a complete refund and qualify for
   a replacement
as soon as I become available

Early findings in the latest version of myself suggest
   the essential idea is sound
There are grounds for optimism and reasons to suggest success
This is a sophisticated product like nothing that has
   been made before
I will turn this around
I will bring a new version of myself
to everyone else

Thoughts and prayers

You are in my thoughts and prayers
With my longing, tears and aching
I'm warning you, its chaos in there
All the ways life has of breaking

You are in my thoughts and prayers
What else am I going to do?
The whisper of your name
It's how I feel for you

You are in my thoughts and prayers
It's hard to make a distinction
It's turning towards some light
It's making you my intention

You are in my thoughts and prayers
I hold your life in mine
The silence where no words
Could ever match this time

You are in my thoughts and prayers
No matter what we believe
Some sacred sign of love and care
Call it solidarity

You are in my thoughts and prayers
When your day has fallen apart
It's just another way to say
I keep you in this heart

Sink

The day begins with a thought
You'd prefer not to have had
A message holding some ballast
All set to sink your heart

Step back and study this thought
The heaviness it contains
The way it looks at you
Daring to drown the day

Lean in, consider it carefully
Bow down, show it respect
You will face each other today
But it doesn't need to be yet

Poem started on a birthday

Sometime before we were, we were conceived
All of a sudden we're here, there's no guarantee
And all our days freighted with uncertainty
After this poem we slip into history

Along the way we become ourselves
(This is much later than when we arrive
But all of this a little undefined)
The person we are to everyone else

Collecting new baggage every day
The stops and starts and acceleration
At night questions about destination
All we let go of, all we give away

Picking up speed, this unlikely flight
Peering out from inside this meteor shower
At sixty-seven thousand miles an hour
Sparkling the dark with our brief, bright light

The days seem to slow, the years to speed up
In this bright field of friendship and forgiveness
Here you stand, quite still, catching your breath
Untroubled by this thought, how long have I got?

Birthday morning, the café buzzing
Here we go again, once more round the sun
Each year missing one more loved one
Sitting here, alone, all of a sudden

Taking my prayers for a walk

Some mornings I take my prayers for a walk
It's good for them to stretch their legs
It helps to clear the head

They run off without me, there's so much going on
Curious, innocent, perhaps a little anxious
Often it's hard for me to keep up

They explore each other, talk amongst themselves
Now and then falling silent
Listening to me and me to them

They may stop me in my tracks, reverse, go back
Where they take me I'll never know
It's not straightforward, even when we get there

My prayers rarely fail to surprise me
They get me out of myself
They don't know what they're capable of

THIS STORY

Tradition

What they passed
To you
Is not what had been passed
To them

What they found
Worked for them
That
Is what they passed to you

And what you are holding
Now
Is not
What they gave you

It is what we make of it
Often
Without knowing it
Even as we hold it

Those who first held this
Now
They wouldn't know it

So we do what they did
Take it up
Hold it
Work with it
Pass it on

Fear not

I heard a voice say fear not
That the morning carries joy
That after the day gives birth to night
The darkness raises light

I saw the dawn break from on high
A light over every life
Each sun and star, each universe
A promise of peace on earth

I heard a voice say fear not
That weeping will not last
That every good and perfect gift
Comes from the place of light

The book

The book wants a word with you
The book wants to hear from you
This is how the book
Keeps itself alive

The book is a conversation
An argument with itself
An argument with you

The book is a version of the book
Which is a version of the book

You can ask the book to instruct you on your sex life
The book would rather not
The book does not feel qualified
Or let the book fall open when you want to make a decision
The book is as baffled as you

If you ask the book the wrong question
The book will give you the wrong answer
The book is not a creed
Will not tell you what to believe
The book may be true
Even when it is mistaken

The book will infuriate, comfort or guide you
The book is a story, unwritten without you
The book may reassure you
You're not the first this has happened to
The book is not about you
The book is all about you

The book wants a word with you
The book wants to hear from you

Gazing at a star (Christmas poem)

The darkening way, the clapped-out vehicle
Maps which draw some adjacent possible

The silent night and never-lasting light
Beatific faces cloaked in plain sight

A rock 'n' roll chorus in lateral flow
A song of history sung from below

Light and dark fist bump, wink, reconcile
Peace and goodwill gazing up from a child

Time shifts on the quiet, nobody notices
Joy pirouettes, leaps on her axis

This time last week, stardust, you and me
Never knew astronomy was our family tree

A far-flung galaxy can still overwhelm
Gazing at a star, talking to yourself

Love can't come down when it's already here
Beside us, inside us, every day of the year

Homeless, undocumented, refugee
Love, the disruptive technology

Slouching, sprinting, looking all around
Any place for Christmas to call home

Ring out the old

Ring out the old, ring in the new
Open the door, future coming through
Stand on a chair, is that the time?
Anyone know the words to Auld Lang Syne?

Look at us all, take in the view
Ring out the old, ring in the new
All those we love, all those not here
This liminal now, measured in tears

While the door's open, let the past out
The daily leap of faith, and doubt
In joy or pain, in sun or rain
Raise a cup of kindness again

Spiritual not religious

We are not church, mosque, synagogue
We are not religious
We are not liturgy, creed, confession
We are not right or wrong

We are not prayer, chant or hymn
We are not peer pressure from the dead
We do not claim to know what all this is
All this *is*, that we are part of

We are paying attention
We are listening to the day
We are wide-eyed to find we are here
We may fall silent

We are love, joy, patience and peace
Gentle, trustworthy, kind and composed
We were never introduced to our own humility
We are spiritual not religious

Epiphany

The answer you weren't looking for
The way you went by mistake
The known unknown you never knew
'Til it was staring you in the face

Arrives just after you give up
No formula or calculation
The star, the sky, the vaguest hunch
No map marks this destination

Emerges slowly as morning
Dawns on you like a new day
As if all your previous light was dark
And all of the dark made this way

How to become an insider

You've seen the building from the road and thought about going in.

You know some regulars who enthuse about what it means to them.

You're in two minds but you need to do something. Perhaps it's worth a try. Just once. To find out.

This is the day. As a trickle of people turn to go in, you walk up to the door.

You feel like an outsider. No-one smiles toward you.

The insiders are preoccupied, preparing for whatever it is they do, inside these walls.

You have second thoughts, third thoughts. Your thoughts get into an argument.

Isn't every insider a recovering outsider? But what if they ask you to do things you don't know how to do? What if you're embarrassed? Found out?

You decide it doesn't matter what people think. (You win the argument.)

At the threshold you breathe in and cross over. You go in.

Is everyone looking at you?

You keep moving until instead of being just inside the inside you are in the middle of the inside.

You look at these strange fixtures and fittings. You look at people's faces. No one is looking at you after all.

You want to try to look like an insider, but how?

One minute people are standing, the next sitting. Or kneeling.

Some people look exhilarated, like they can do anything. Others just stand there, as if they're trying to remember why they came.

Some people are raising their hands. Some are singing, their mouths opening and closing on a tune you don't know, on words you can't make out.

No-one has noticed you aren't in step with the choreography. You seem to have blended in. This is not as bad as you'd imagined.

Perhaps being here will be good for you. Everyone seems to have this faith.

All these people who crossed that threshold before you. These people who found a place to belong.

You select Level 1.

The treadmill moves and you begin to jog. You take it up a notch.

Level 2.

You look up and around. All these faces.

You breathe in. You breathe out.

You're an insider.

Forty (Poem in Lent)

At winter's end it may begin
The sun is low, we long for spring

The daily quest, the wrong direction
A forty-day course correction

Apply the brakes and turn around
Set the satnav to stranger ground

The sign is drawn upon the forehead
Quite soon it seems we'll all be dead

While holding on and letting go
We enter the fast where we slow

Look up, look out and look inside
Find the lit bush then turn aside

A light still burns in all this darkness
Joy and grief in this bright sadness

The calendar, a sacred circle
Winding threads in the colour purple

easter revolution

the easter revolution will not be televised
it is not captured on cctv because it is captured in the heart
it is not a big event in history
(it is too big for history ... and also too small)
the easter revolution is a beautiful disguise
it is brought to you by a woman in a flowing green dress,
facing down
the riot police
and a shirtsleeved man standing before a line of tanks
but also in the patience of the person serving you
on the supermarket checkout
and the devotion of your neighbour to her child,
the one people name
different
it is brought to you by those who are seldom heard
and routinely
overlooked
in the fields, someone picking coffee
on the sea, someone in an exodus
and in the forest, a nun, gunned down
for protecting the trees, while reciting the Beatitudes
'we're not burying you,' say her fellow revolutionaries at the
funeral, 'we're planting you'

no-one notices as the subtle bud rises quietly from dark earth
or as someone, turning away from the powers that be, kneels
to write something, lower case, in the sand
it is the quietest sound, this revolution,
it is almost not there
like that everflowing stream
somewhere
not far from here

the easter revolution takes no-one by force
except the force of love
which is no force at all
and the greatest force of all
it is the revolution we long for
but can't quite name
the one that is undated because it is every date that ever was
the one that is usually unseen but always
at every moment
hiding in plain sight

Church noticeboards

(In Glasgow I passed a church where their noticeboard read: 'Open. Inclusive. Welcoming.' Perhaps some other communities might like some help with their own noticeboards.)

Closed. Exclusive. Intimidating.

Falling Over. Helping Each Other Up. Falling Over.

Elitist. Impenetrable. Not for You.

Singing. Can. Help.

Homophobic. Misogynist. Smiling.

Trying. Our. Best.

Damp. Dark. Disappointing.

Finally. Some. Quiet.

Please. Don't. Interrupt.

We. Don't. Know. Either.

Preserving. The. Past.

Making. It Up. Together.

Biblical. When. It Suits.

Religion. Is. Politics.

Priest

You're standing there for us
We're standing here for you
Love always stands with us
Stands for, stands in, stands up

Your hands, they welcome life
And death, that's cradled too
They sign some absolution
For all, for me, for you

Attentive as the poet
To the cadence of the day
The rhyme scheme of a life
We're born, we live, we die

We're born, we live, we die
You hold our secret life
Devices and desires
Repent, repair, renew

We're each a sacrament
Reverent upon this earth
Divining bread and wine
In them, in him, in her

Holding holy orders
Vested in unseen light
Each new day's forgiveness
Morning, noon and night

You're standing there for us
We're standing here for you
Love always stands with us
Stands for, stands in, stands up

Retreat

All in deep quiet, this singing tree
Boughs reaching out, over you and me
Sunlight and shadow, signing the day
Asking myself if this is how to pray

Becoming as nothing, this window pane
Keeping at bay, the wind and the rain
Taken for granted, existing between
Playing invisible, scene and unseen

Barefoot, walking, carrying a child
Set on this shelf, eighteen inches high
Something about her feels like a sign
Made up from nothing, something divine

Paper and pen, scratching retreat
These words, these lines, phone out of reach
Out of the quiet, something is heard
Soon after in the beginning, was the word

The day the weeks meet

The priest stands to begin
She carries with her most of the week
The days she has been preparing to stand here

Under stole and chasuble, Psalm and Gospel
Read and reread, those connections across time
How they will speak to everyone as she stands here

Cosmic themes in hymns, ringing in her mind
How they sing this festival, its ancient rhyme
And amplify this faith as she stands here

The anecdote and analogy, the sermon
Exposition, application, ebb and flow
(Is it concentration, how those eyes have closed?)

The holy monologue of great thanksgiving
The bread broken, the wine outpoured, hands held high
The drama as she stands here for you or me

Mrs Jones wanders in late, her mind, like her phone,
Unsilenced, she carries with her most of the week
The days she has thought mainly about surviving

The phone goes off during the first reading
The second mentions a Philip and her mind
Goes to the man she was married to

In the hymn, still thinking of him,
She sees a child, about the age her daughter
Would have been, if she had lived

Wiping her eyes, she doesn't notice as the priest
Rises with words of peace, and some muscle memory
Carries her from her seat, carries her week

Into this crooked line of wounded souls
Queuing to survive. She may stay for coffee
The drama as she stands here, for you or me

More

You are difficult to describe
In the words we have found so far
You are more
Than
You are both
And

We anthropomorphise you
Although, for the most part
We cannot see
Our
Selves

You are not binary
We say we are made
In your image

THIS END

A quiet word

Can you let me know when I start
Becoming like that?
When I no longer hear myself
Or see myself
When I don't notice as everyone else
Looks away from me,
At everyone else,
As they send those glances,
The kind I once glanced to you,
About someone else

Can you take me aside
And have a quiet word
When I start becoming like that?
When I have moved from the funny
Inappropriate
To the inappropriate
Inappropriate
Which is not funny
For anyone
Can you take me aside
And have a quiet word?
And if I resist
Can you persist?

Can you point me to the edit button
When I'm going on too long
When I'm on send
But not on receive
And apparently believe
It's all about me?
When I'm thinking too much
Of myself again
Can you have a quiet word?
Can you gently take me down?

Elastic snap

I'm looking up, flat on the pitch
You're all looking down at me
That life, before this sudden twist
The world, like a ball, at my feet

I read the game, I saw the space
I wasn't fouled, I wasn't kicked
I had the pass, the time and place
The fall to earth, I didn't see this

Was it a pop? Was it a crack?
The sound as my season ended
Inside leg, an elastic snap
Age greets me, demands surrender

I'm looking up, in plastered leg
Achilles tendon ruptured
My world contracted to this bed
This field of dreams, interrupted.

Spring

In
Spring
I
Visit
Mum
In
Winter

Taking mum to the doctor

How am I? Well, a lot of things I can't do now
I get on with it but, my speech, well, you know
That's a setback, and I can't go out on my own
I might fall down, when I'm all alone

Looking at your scans, there's accelerating shrinkage
Speech, memory, balance, this explains your symptoms
Will you get better? I'm afraid I don't think so
But we have some more tablets, the shrinkage might slow

How am I? I'm old! I doubt I'll recover
All my life I've been a nurse, I look after others
At my age, well, things do get in a muddle
More tablets? Let's leave it. It can't be that harmful

Hazardous

I'm sure I used to be good at this
Thinking the thought, then framing it

Now I seem to get it all wrong
No sooner it's left my tongue

My words appear to change their meaning
The second before they meet your hearing

The question I raised was innocent
It metamorphosed into criticism

I honestly never thought you'd hear that
Wait, stop, let me take it all back

Do we travel any more hazardous journey
Than the one between you and me

One in the morning

This one in the morning and this one at night
And each time the thought, have I got this right?
Another, hard to swallow, keeps my joints in motion
This drink I make, sorts the digestion

The latest novel exercise, a trip to the gym
Need to walk a bit faster, be more disciplined
A rumble and a grumble I want to dismiss
They've got a clever camera, 'Can you pee in this?'

The who I am is wearing out, the what I am is breaking
And now they need to take this out, and this will need replacing
And then the seismic moment comes out of the blue
It's been a good run, but what can you do?

I've had some kind of acronym, a string of strange words
Now I'm on a pathway, 'No way back to where you were.
You've had a one-off episode, which wants to be a series
Three times daily, take two of these.'

It's management now, remember this, remember that
As time turns us all into hypochondriacs
Watch your constitution, lose a bit of weight
Hold yourself together, with this gaffer tape

The body's conversation in the middle of the night
Impolite reminder of the dimming of the light
Then a quieter voice, as if my soul replies,
I'm glad to be here, I'm glad to be alive.

Home from home

You look familiar, are we related?
Sorry to be cross, I do get frustrated
Are you my brother, no, you're my father?
Isn't it funny? I'll be fine in an hour

This feels all wrong, doing this with you
It was always you, taking me to the loo
Our earliest truth, all your care for us
When we were upset and powerless

I can't find the word, the place, the name
Your questions a searchlight inside my brain
The carers are kind but it's all getting worse
Someone broke in last night, took my purse

WhatsApp messages overtake each other
As we become parents to fathers or mothers
Hello, can you hear me? we shout down the phone
Call the GP, call the bank, who knows the pin code?

Is that an ambulance over the road?
Bill's back to hospital, we're all so old
The telly's on loud, I can't really see
It passes the time, it's company

You were the can-do woman but now you can't
You reach for a word like you're lost in a trance
Your superpowers no more present
Caught in a sentence that makes no sense

I can't get up, I've rung the alarm
I'm flat on the floor, I'm losing my calm
You're all very kind, you're doing your best
I've packed my case, you all need a rest

The humiliation, the rage, the crying
The pathetic indignity of ageing and dying
Your body and mind now spent and shrinking
Yet, still, now and then, that light inside burning

Cradling your hand, this final gaze
Our end will not rewrite our days
Breathe out, let go, goodbye, see you, mum
Breathe in, take hold, hello, grandson

My back has gone

My back has gone and left no forwarding address
No notice, no goodbye, just upped and left
We're strolling along, all fine, I turn, it's gone
Or, rising from my seat, off goes the alarm

Is it the back of beyond, for which it leaves so abruptly?
Are there notices on the wall for yoga and osteopathy?
Is it standing room only, with meetings back-to-back?
Is it a safe space, has someone always got your back?

Meanwhile I'm left stooping, not so proud, not so straight
These tentative movements, this peculiar gait
I miss the back's support in this elasticated brace
The news that I've lost it, advertised on my face

Now I get to meet this body, as each foot hits the ground
Shooting pain reminders that the back must be found
When the back goes it leaves us crooked and provisional
And a whole new perspective from which we get to view this all.

Affronted

In the hotel at breakfast an older man and a younger woman
Approach the empty table, between me and the next guy.
Without looking up from my boiled egg
I see him stop, think twice, then turn away
We don't want to sit with the old folk,
I hear him say.

On the Tube a middle-aged woman
Jumps up from her seat, points it out to me
(I already know it's a seat)
She must be offering it to some deserving elder
Someone I cannot quite see
Although, for some reason, she's looking at me
How offensive an act of kindness
Can be. She has no idea
How old I really feel

At a bar in America they are asking for ID
But tonight I've forgotten
To bring my passport with me
I mentally prepare my apology
But here comes my drink
– the cheek of it –
The waiter doesn't ask me anything.
I'm affronted to be wearing
Proof of my age
On this face, I can't see
All day, every day

I see you've got new shoes,
My friend observes
– about to jeopardise that status –
They look very comfortable
My dad used to have shoes like that.

What are we going to do?

What are we going to do with our differences?
Now that we harbour these grudges
Will we brush them aside or talk about it?
Our competing versions of justice

That thing you said, the way I behaved
The genie that jumped from the bottle
I let you down, you gave me up
Can this knot ever be untangled?

It is what it is, is what everyone says
But what if it's not what it seems?
If I moved to you, would you move to me?
So what was won't define what will be

Unlock

We said I do, we meant it too
Please don't judge me, I won't judge you

We spoke the words, from deep in our hearts
But life in time called us apart

Richer, poorer, better or worse
Solemn vows, we couldn't make work

We lived with loss, we carried shame
Tried to deny it, disguised the pain

Our faith in each other turned to dust
The fury, the rage, we're all cried out

This weight inside, we lay it down
Regrets that spin around and around

Mainly it's sad, occasionally funny
Except when we have to talk about money

We've signed the forms that mark a new start
How long does it take to rewire a heart?

Release the lock, untangle the knot
Turn the key to unlock the wedlock

Two became one, now one becomes two
I'll be a new me, you'll be a new you

This is our prayer, let it be so
To have and to hold and now to let go

Lowering

If we want people to be raised well
Then let us also be lowered well
To lower someone
In the way we would wish to be lowered
To lower them with love and respect

To let them down kindly
Firmly sometimes, but tenderly
Always being trustworthy
Learning when to hold someone
When to release them

To let the cords loosen in your grip
To let the body lie there in the good earth
To stand quietly in the universe
To send them on their way
To go on yours

Same seat as you

You never got to meet
But she sat here too
Same route, same seat as you

Same luggage, the surprise
At being alive
The ache
That someone died

Even though she left
Before you got on
The seat is still warm

Even though she left
This pew
A hundred years ago

Seven blessings when you lose someone you love
(A funeral poem)

1.
Blessed is this earth, beneath our feet (the only one we have)

2.
This being here, this breath, this air,
This human family, this love we share

3.
Blessed are we all in our doubt and disbelief
The lonely path as we carry our grief
Holding this heartache, this hard-to-believe

4.
Blessed all the hours when we were side by side
Runs past so soon, this river of time
The entangled days of rows and laughs
We hold on to each other, deep in our hearts

5.
Blessed every soul who is no longer here
Siblings, parents, sons and daughters,
Wives, husbands, partners, lovers
Friends we have loved, all who we miss
This love that makes our life what it is

6.
Blessed be their presence, also their absence
Blessed be this sorrow and reluctant acceptance
Blessed be their memory in tears, in smiles
How they return to us, once in a while
Blessed our regret, what we left unsaid
Peace upon the living, peace upon the dead

7.
Blessed is this earth beneath our feet
This house of light in the great dark night
Every life of kindness, every day till we die
Blessed are those lives we no longer see
The ones who were with us and still never leave
Blessed is the love that holds us together
To have and to hold, for ever and ever

Alive

In answer to your question –
the one you have taken to asking recently –
I can only apologise.
When you ask how it feels –
and I know you are about to say,
now that you are a grandfather –
I cannot find my feelings.
I do not deliver
The joy-of-joy lit-up-face
That you were anticipating.
I'm not sure what it feels like.

But yesterday as I felt
Your soft round head lying
Inside the palm of my hand
And felt your breath, in out
In out, on my shoulder
And heard you hum along
In your sleep
To a song only you could hear
Then, for a moment, little person
Before I carefully handed you back –
into the hands once handed to
me – I felt your life in my life
And all life in every life
And that's how I knew
How I feel.

I feel alive.

Scattering

We scattered your ashes
Your earthly remains

We blinked away tears
Still holding the pain

The wind gave us all
A sudden surprise

Blowing you everywhere
Lifting you high

Is this who you are
Flecked, grey and white

Jumping the breeze
To shoes and tights?

But how can a face
Smile as it cries?

How can you be in dust
When you are in us?

The light we shared (A parting poem)

We first lit this light
And found it lit a shared way

As we held this light
We thought it was for always

In time, this light lit up
A parting in the way

From this light we shared
We now each take new light

As this light we held goes dark
We hold these two lights

The light is not dimmed
It lights our different ways

Fall

Umber, ochre, yellow, brown
Down they fall, without comment
Onto us, we do not notice
Onto field and pavement

Each tree unmoved, reveals no grief
No ritual or obituary
Each relative released with ease
Each leaving its own ceremony

All golden now, most fallen
December now, year ending
The darkness now, makes its own light
After this great descending

Gone

They're gone now
Into the night
Darkness
Misleading our sight

They still hold us
As we hold them
All of us held
In some other light

Sign of the peace

Over the top of the train seat
You peer back at me, I peer toward you
You are new here, I may not be safe
Your long journey has been hazardous
You do not speak our language
I have a distant memory of your country
I raise my eyebrows, stretch my lips wide
This is a sign of the peace, this is a smile
I squash my face into a ridiculous shape
Look into your eyes, will you also make a sign?
Instead you look past me, at a new unknown
Someone waving at you, their hand raised high
Lips stretched, face squashed, forehead in a crease
The daily human call on all of us
To share a sign of the peace

THIS HOME

Life writing

In the morning, I make a plan
The outline of a life
A sketch of this new day

Next I look among words
For the right one to say
To the characters on my way

Later, now a new scene,
I'm listening, holding my tongue
Waiting for your story to unfold

At times I'm blocked, or clueless
Then events rush, twists and turns
I could never have imagined

In the evening I edit this latest draft
Of myself. What can I develop?
What belongs in someone else's story?

Catch

You prepare your equipment, what you will need
Feel for the weather, beyond the door, what to wear
Then the journey, to the place where you struck lucky before
Here it is, now, cast out and believe
Sit, against the evidence, watch, hope, wait

Each morning this week, sitting here like this
Unspooling my patience, looking for a sign
Once, twice, a faint tug on the line
Flash of silver, below surface of sight
But not a bite, until this, which
I have already thrown back

Why the rule?

Why the rule, that a poem,
Once published, is fixed
And final, as if it has died?
When really, it is new born
Suddenly alive, sensing its
Own limitations, its longing
Deep inside to become itself
Awake to being this work
In progress, like you, like me
Isn't poetry always in motion
Always about to make life
From life? Every time
It crawls unsteadily
Off the page, and climbs
Into your mind

Stand

We know why we're here and also we don't
Conscience brought us here, justice and hope
Is anyone watching, will anyone think again?
Do all of our views add up to anything?

The speakers speak, back here we can't hear them
The PA is bust, there's a lot of cheering
We chant and we sing and vote with our feet
But no-one is elected in this ballot of the street

A march is not predictable with cause and effect
But being human is to say we all connect
And moving so slowly in this great crush
We are learning to speak a new version of us

Kettled, arrested, choosing not to be cowed
Silenced, cancelled, protest disallowed
The future thanks you, strange kind of reward
Freedom disguised in your criminal record

This is us and this is the world we believe in
In other people's shoes we become human beings
This is our protest, this is our free speech
We stand for a world that's just out of reach

Our view of this earth, of all we can see
Depends on where we stand, who we want to be
We are here and now, we are bearing witness
We are asking history to be better than this

Each time we march a path is made
A route through history, a desire way
Let's go, let's get this protest in motion
Who knows, this might be our quiet revolution

Candle

It does not dazzle
It has no beam
And, if it burns fierce,
It soon disappears

It draws you in like a spell
A flickering invitation
To read by it is always
To be open to interpretation

You may gather around it
As it translates the air
As it dances in your eyes
And burns like a prayer

Like the light inside you
It waxes and wanes
And may still surprise
Even when nothing remains

Your light has set
Another alight
Their light
Enlightens you

Warmth

We are connected
Though we have never met
You owe me nothing
But leave me this gift
I feel you here
Though now you are gone
My life and your life
We are one
The warmth on this bus seat
Of your recently departed bum

The fix

In the end
We must fix ourselves
But if
Each of us
Is all of us
In the end
We will all be fixed
By each other

Guidance
(With thanks RW & LW)

A way to get there
This left, then right
Drawn to a shortcut
Ignoring your advice

So now I'm here
In this cul-de-sac
Expecting the furies
Behind my back

Instead, recalculating
Try this, then that
Infinite forgiveness
Of the holy satnav

No condemnation
Now I dread
Long as you guide me
On every road ahead

This is a poem about death

After you have fallen asleep
For the last time
You will wake again
For the first time
You may not know
Where this is
Where you are
But you will hear a familiar voice
'Thank you for your patience.
You are moving forward in the queue
And will be answered as soon as possible …'

Almost nothing

It happens, almost always
As you sit there
Up to your neck in the deep pool
Of your distractions
Eyes drawn this way
And that, each leaping
Shimmering attraction.

(Perhaps) if you close your eyes
These waters might still
(Briefly) as almost everything
Loses interest in you
Now (possibly) almost nothing
Will happen, so that when you open
Them again, everything (maybe)
Begins to move more slowly as
Almost nothing continues
To happen
For a while.

As almost nothing
Is the same
For a while.

Life, a customer satisfaction survey

On a scale of 1-10, how satisfied are you with the days you were given?

Did life meet your expectations?

Excluding the essentials – food, security, shelter, Netflix – which feature of your mortal coil did you find most valuable? Choose from the following:

Family/friendship/love/music/stories/drinking/affirmation/winning/someone listening/it's private – mind your own business.

Which feature was least valuable?

What upgrade would you like to see in the next version of life?:

Additional advice on why we are here/less cruel disease/less cruelty/improved communication with non-human life/improved communication with human life/improved ability to take it all in/additional advice on what happens afterwards.

How would you rate the effectiveness of life's customer services? Was the customer service representative a friend or stranger, a neighbour or nurse, an angel or devil, a composite of these, none of the above?

How long did you wait for a reply when you prayed?:

Five minutes/five hours/five years/still waiting/didn't realise you had to wait.

From the following options, please rank your preferred way to contact a customer service representative:

Dreaming/crying/solitude/singing/dancing/friendship/sex/ running/walking/sitting down/doing something for nothing/the kindness of strangers/the forgiveness of those who know you/birdsong/the company of a cat/the loyalty of a dog/a strong drink.

Overall, would you say life is a rewarding experience and good value for the time required?

Strongly agree/agree/neither agree nor disagree/disagree/strongly disagree/rapidly losing interest/you've lost me completely.

Did you find life provided effective and comprehensive instructions?

Is life easier to use than its competitors?

Did life help you achieve your goals?

On a scale of extremely likely to extremely unlikely, would you recommend life to someone who is considering it?

How would you feel if you had to stop using our product?

Call it

You can call it by another name
Call it a breath held, then held some more
Or your gaze, holding that one face
Call it an incantation that reminds you this is now
Call it thanks, call it help
Call it ordinary astonishment
Call it your feet in someone else's shoes
Or that song, when we all join in
Call it all the trouble you're in
Call it the loss or grief
Or the nearby heaven
We rarely stop to see
It doesn't matter what you call it
But don't ignore it
Call it by another name
Call it anyway

Psalm 23 (remix)

The Lord is our politician.
She stands for election – of all the people all of the time.
She stands for love.
She wants to guide us from the divided bad
   to the common good.
She would like to lead us to green pastures
but knows that we can only go there together.
Her party is the party of the earth and all her creatures.
Her manifesto is peace.
The Lord does not belong to any political party.
The Lord our politician belongs to those who believe
   they do not belong.
The Lord is only in power when the Lord is in service.
The Lord knows that politics is working when goodness
   and mercy follow the people
all the days of their life.

(Psalm for a) home

May your doorbell ring with a welcome
your home keep a couch for the weary
and your table hold a space for those
out of place

May the kettle in the kitchen be just boiled
your living room rock with laughter
and your phone be sometimes out of reach

May your clothes be handed on
your plants remind you to water them
and the compost bin become your daily sermon

May your car give people lifts
(may your neighbours' names be known)
and your carbon footprint be gentle
whatever the road that rises to meet you

May you cherish each quiet space
and the paths you take into each day

May goodness and mercy follow you
down each and every way.

Listen now!

On today's episode, two new parents
Are pushing buggies past you, laughing
In disbelief at their lack of sleep
We have music from Stevie Wonder
Floating towards you from the open door
Of that café, where a green-eyed husky
Has ordered a bowl of water and an oat
Cappuccino for the guy he's taking for a walk

Also in this episode we're delighted to welcome back
Spring, a regular visitor to the show at this time of year
She'll be introducing us to the dappled light
Falling through the tree you're now walking under
And talking about her long-running campaign
To bring life out of death

You don't need to save, like or download
This episode, there'll be another one
Along in a minute
You'll find us on all the usual platforms
As well as pavements, cycle paths
Country lanes, high streets and seaside strolls

Subscription is free but to hear this episode
You'll need to remove your earbuds or
Take off your headphones
Listen now!

Thankful

For those of us present
Gathered here
Those unseen who bring
All this we share

For those we carry
Into this space and time
The ones we hold
In heart and mind

This earth from which we're raised
This path on which we travel
All the sorrow, all the praise
For all of this we're thankful

THIS LIFE
(SOME AFTERWORDS)

Hanging in a stairwell rising above the cloisters of Iona Abbey is a print of a painting held in Edinburgh's National Gallery. *Saint Bride*, by the Scottish artist John Duncan, was painted in the early 20th century and I've looked at it on my way up those stairs a hundred times over thirty-five years.

It captures a story about the Irish saint – usually known as Bridget – as she's transported by angels across the earth to Bethlehem on her mission to act as Mary's midwife at the birth of Jesus.

Bridget, who is thought to have died in 525, is being flown back to the beginning of what we call the first century. High in the air she is attended by seagulls and below, in the choppy Hebridean waters, by seals.

The outline of Iona Abbey is visible in the background, although Columba didn't wash up on Iona from Ireland until 563 AD, while building on the Abbey was not begun until 1200 AD.

Stories, like paintings or poems, feel no need to stick to the rules of space and time. Nor do saints, which I tried to capture in **Call the midwife**, a poem about Bridget, given a cultural peg in the 21st century.

While most of these poems first showed up in Broccoli, a little coffee shop run by my friend Charlie, near the home of Arsenal Football Club, and the place I visit for my daily quiet time, a good number emerged on Iona. *Lectio Divina* (Divine Reading) is an imaginative, go-slow approach to reading sacred writing which might go back to the sixth-century Italian monk Benedict. Staying on Iona fourteen centuries later, Dr Ute Susanna Molitor, Presbyterian minister and Eco-Spiritual Director, introduced us to the practice of *Terra Divina* (Divine Earth). Contemplating the ground as sacred text gave rise to **Terra Divina (William Blake remix)** and to other poems, including **Grumbling**, set in the ruins of the island's Hermit's Cell.

The solitude required for a poem to become itself helps me orientate myself in a way that the app on my phone will never understand when it asks me if it's OK to use my location, 'just now or always' **(Location)**. But the stop-start-scrap-that-and-start-again attempt to form a poem helps me audit my life. The daily discipline with pen and notebook persuades me to look twice at time, to focus in on a detail **(Detectorist)** or pull back the lens on a scene I hadn't seen. The poem **Now** was inspired by *Perfect Days*, a film by Wim Wenders. Cycling over a bridge at day's end, and asked what's happening tomorrow, Hirayama, the central character, turns to his niece, 'Next time is next time, and now is now.'

The quiet joy of company may hold the strength we need to endure the day or the comedy to laugh at it: the companionship of a long-time partner (**My third marriage**); or a gallery of paintings haunted by long-gone painters (**Old friends**); the common purpose of activists and agitators (**Stand, Everyday election**); or the company of what one writer called 'a great cloud of witnesses' which inform poems like **Taking my prayers for a walk, Call it** or **Thoughts and prayers**.

I wrote **Assembly** after sitting in a Zoom meeting with global practitioners of Citizens' Assemblies, at the invitation of a posse of artists and agitators called Hard Art. This offbeat band of writers, filmmakers, playwrights, musicians and actors emerged as a creative response to 'climate and democratic collapse'. Not evidently 'religious', it's surprised me how often the conversation in these monthly gatherings turns to a longing for shared ritual or community beyond a peer group.

Religions are onto something when they aren't trying to control everyone, but for many of us their traditions, once a useful map to navigate a life, have given up their holy ghost. Some of the poems in this collection respond to festivals like Christmas or Epiphany or to what we found handed to us by those who came before (**The book, Tradition, The day the weeks meet**).

The poem **easter revolution** was written after the singer-songwriter Garth Hewitt asked if I could come up with some liner notes for his 2023 album of the same name.

I wrote **Priest** at the invitation of Mark Oakley, now Dean of Southwark Cathedral but probably its bard, to mark the thirtieth anniversary of his becoming a priest. *'Attentive as the poet/To the cadence of the day/The rhyme scheme of a life/We're born, we live, we die ...'*

One day a month I disappear into an unlikely urban nest in east London called the Royal Foundation of St Katharine. **Retreat** arrived while I was staring at a tree through the window, trying and failing, as usual, to pray.

What would **Church noticeboards** say if they told the truth about the values held by those who meet in the buildings towering behind them? This thought came to me passing a church in Glasgow where the noticeboard proclaimed, strikingly: *'Open. Inclusive. Welcoming.'*

Slowly, in the face of hostility and fear, new traditions emerge. **The light we shared (A parting poem)** was kindled during a separation ceremony in 1999 at St Luke's Church in Holloway, north London, led by the Rev. Dave Tomlinson. After a year of sometimes heartbreaking reflection, two good friends had decided their marriage had reached an end. They wanted to part publicly, just as they had come together publicly, standing within a community of friendship which had travelled with them and shared their story. Dave led a ritual in which three candles stood on a table with only the central one lit. The couple, marking the end of this relationship, approached the table and each lit one of the unlit candles from the central candle. Dave blew out the central candle. It seems strange that religions rarely create ceremonies for the times when life goes wrong – with the exception of funerals.

One enduring tradition is the tradition of festival and I wrote **Tent** to mark the fiftieth appearance of the Greenbelt Arts Festival, to which I have been making pilgrimage every August since I was seventeen.

Can any of us be as old as we're told we are? Many of the later poems in this book capture the effect of time on space or of the years on the body.

Poems in the section 'Letting Go' are found carrying a broken body around the day (**Elastic snap, One in the morning**) or carrying an ageing relative to the latest medical appointment or through some new bewilderment (**Home from Home**). Or carrying a loved one on a final journey (**Lowering, Scattering, Fall, Gone**).

I would love to live, riffing on a tiny jewel of a poem by the late John O'Donohue, was written for the departure of Jean Willson, in honour of her husband Norman and daughter Tara. **Seven blessings when you lose someone you love (A funeral poem)** is a companion piece to **Seven blessings for a wedding**, which appeared in my earlier collection *Julian of Norwich's Teabag*.

New people arrive as others make their leave and **Alive** was inspired after two little people, Ari and Leo, showed up in our worlds, thanks to their parents, our children. People asked what it felt like to have become a grandfather and I didn't know until I'd written a poem about it.

Time leaves you **Thankful** if you find time to think about it.

SOURCES AND ACKNOWLEDGEMENTS

'Fluent', by John O'Donohue, from *Conomara Blues: Poems*, Transworld Publishers, 2001. Used by permission of Ann Cahill, Director, John O'Donohue Literary Estate.

Wild Goose Publications, the publishing house of the Iona Community established in the Celtic Christian tradition of Saint Columba, produces books, e-books, CDs and digital downloads on:

- holistic spirituality
- social justice
- political, peace and environmental issues
- healing and wellbeing
- innovative approaches to worship
- song in worship, including the work of the Wild Goose Resource Group
- material for meditation and reflection

Visit our website at
www.ionabooks.com
for details of all our products and online sales